Estate Planning for Catholics

A Guide to Doing God's Will in Your Will
(and Other Estate Planning Documents)

Salvatore J. LaMendola

authorHOUSE®

AuthorHouse™
1663 Liberty Drive
Bloomington, IN 47403
www.authorhouse.com
Phone: 1 (800) 839-8640

Published by AuthorHouse 03/16/2018

ISBN: 978-1-5462-3319-0 (sc)
ISBN: 978-1-5462-3318-3 (e)

Library of Congress Control Number: 2018903281

Print information available on the last page.

Cover Art: Francis Renounces His Paternal Inheritance, Stripping off His Clothes before the Bishop of Assisi, Giotto Di Bondone (1266–1337). See chapter 7 for more on renouncement (or disclaimer) planning.

This book is meant to educate and assist readers. It is not meant to give legal advice. It speaks neither in the name of the Roman Catholic Church nor in the name of the author's law firm. This book is not intended as a substitute for the advice of a qualified estate planning professional or tax specialist. The author and publisher shall have neither liability nor responsibility to any person or entity with respect to any loss or damage caused or alleged to be caused, directly or indirectly, by the information contained in this book.

DOUAY-RHEIMS 1899 AMERICAN EDITION (DRA)
Scriptures were taken from the Douay-Rheims 1899 American Edition of The Bible - Public Domain.

Contents

Contents

Mariae, Matri Dei, et Mei

Acknowledgment

The author is most grateful to Mrs. Kathleen Plumb, editor and publisher of *The Four Marks* (www.thefourmarks.com), without whose patronage and encouragement this book would not have been completed.

Introduction

Therefore, whether you eat or drink,
or whatsoever else you do,
do all to the glory of God.
—1 Corinthians 10:31

Does your estate plan give glory to God? Or does it ignore Him completely as most do:

> According to many surveys, 95+ percent of Americans believe in God or some type of higher power, yet few estate plans address any aspect of religion, or a particular philosophical attitude. This inadequacy has tremendous personal impact, because no area of the law is more fraught with religious issues than estate planning. If you endeavored to live your life in conformity with your religious beliefs, then your final medical decisions, funeral

arrangements, and distributions under your
will should be consistent with those beliefs.[1]

If it ignores Him completely, use this book to change that.
It was written to help you do God's Will in your Will[2] (and
other estate planning documents).

---

[1] Martin M. Shenkman, Esq., 2007 ABA Leadership Conference
Outline, *Religion and Estate Planning*.

[2] Unless otherwise noted, what is said about last will and testaments
(or "wills" for short) in this book applies to revocable living trusts
(or "living trusts" for short). Nowadays the job of describing who
gets what, when, and how at death is commonly given to the living
trust rather than the will. When a living trust is used, the will's role
is reduced to merely delivering (or "pouring over") to the living trust
all assets (if any) that may have fallen into the deceased's probate
estate (usually because of an oversight). Wills that are so coordinated
with living trusts are called "pour-over" wills. Why is the word
"living" in revocable living trust? It's present to indicate that these
types of trusts come into existence when the settlor is still living (as
opposed to testamentary trusts, which come into existence under a
will at the testator's death). "Living" could also validly be applied
to *irrevocable* trusts that come into existence when the settlor is still
living. However, the convention is to use "living" only in connection
with trusts that are both set up during the settlor's lifetime *and* that
are *revocable* as well.

CHAPTER 1

The Health Care
Proxy: Before Death

See ye that I alone am, and there is no other God besides Me:
I will kill and I will make to live.
—Deuteronomy 32:39

Since the greatest gift we have from God is life itself, it makes
sense to start with the estate planning document that deals
with end-of-life issues—the Health Care Proxy. Unfortunately,
this document goes by many other names, including "Advance
Directive," "Medical Power of Attorney," and "Designation
of Health Care Surrogate." Yet the common element of all
of them is the establishment of an agency relationship. This
means that if you are too ill to communicate your health care
wishes to your doctors, your agent steps into your shoes to
speak for you.

Though your wishes could be transmitted to your agent
orally, the better practice is to write them down. At this point,
it important to distinguish the Health Care Proxy from the
Living Will. While the Living Will also contains written wishes
concerning care, it *does not* create an agency relationship. For

this reason, the Health Care Proxy is the far superior approach. With today's fast-changing technology, it is much better to appoint someone to decide what to do based on circumstances as they present themselves in the future than to attempt to predict those future circumstances now and try to instruct accordingly.[3]

Who should be your agent and backup agent? Choose people who are not only prudent decision makers but who also possess a healthy dose of fortitude. Catholicism's teachings on the value of suffering and on the value of human life (no matter what its quality) are very much at odds with today's medical establishment. You may need your agent to resort to the courts to get your doctors to comply. A direction to your agent to take legal action to protect your rights and best interests is probably worth including in your document.

When it comes to health care instructions, the health of your immortal soul takes first priority. It is a dogma of the Church that only those dying in the state of sanctifying grace have a claim to the inheritance of heaven. Thus, requesting the last sacraments in a Health Care Proxy is essential. Naming the priest whom you would like to administer the last sacraments is also a good idea (with a backup named too). Including information on how to contact the priest (his address, phone number, etc.) also makes sense.

Women of childbearing age should include an instruction in their Health Care Proxies to maintain their own lives for as long as possible for the sake of the child. Numerous women who have been clinically brain dead have given birth months after being so diagnosed. A request for baptism and

---

[3] Since "do not resuscitate" orders (DNRs) and physician orders for life-sustaining treatment (POLSTs) work the same as Living Wills, they should *supplement* a Health Care Proxy, not *supplant* one.

confirmation for the child in case of complications is also a very good idea.

Asking to be provided with sacramentals (crucifix, rosary, enrollment in confraternity of the brown scapular, etc.) also makes sense. Requests for assistance in gaining the plenary indulgence at the hour of death and for prayers of family and friends for the grace of final perseverance are also highly recommended.

When it comes to the body, suffering and pain-relieving medication should be addressed. A statement in a Health Care Proxy offering up one's suffering in satisfaction for one's sins, the sins of others, and other worthy intentions (the conversion of family members, the relief of members of the Church Suffering, etc.) is a great idea. In this way, you will avoid squandering illness.[4]

It is okay to request heavy doses of pain-relieving medication (such as morphine) in a Health Care Proxy so long as the medication is not being used as a *cover* for euthanasia. With that said, pain-relieving medication should be moderated for the sake of worthy reception of the last sacraments. For the more heroic who wish to better follow the example of our Lord's passion, a request for minimal or no pain medication may be appropriate.[5]

Of course, a request for euthanasia (suicide) is totally out of bounds. There is no dignity in a death that puts one in hell forever, and there is no compassion in encouraging people to choose eternal over temporal suffering.

---

[4] This comes from the prayer book for the hospitalized by Frs. Rumble and Carty, *Why Squander Illness?*

[5] It is recorded in Matthew 27:34 ("wine … mingled with gall") and in Mark 15:23 ("wine mingled with myrrh") that our Lord refused this pain-relieving drug when it was offered to Him.

At this point, it would be good to distinguish between active and passive euthanasia. Most of us recognize the wrongfulness of active euthanasia, such as lethal injection (or death by commission). But under certain circumstances, passive euthanasia (or death by omission) can be just as wrong. One of the best examples of this is the case of Terri Schiavo.[6] Proper instruction in a Health Care Proxy should guard against both.[7] You should anticipate the possibility that your situation may be too hard for your agent to handle. You should include a provision instructing the agent to consult a good moral theologian in that case.

For those interested in organ donation, *brain death* (whether partial or full) is false death and should not be used as the criterion of when the soul has left the body. The onset of putrefaction remains the true criterion.[8] Cardiac death, circulatory death, and other inventions should also be avoided as criteria. Many good Catholic authors have written on this.[9] They point out how false *brain death* is being used to rationalize murder so that vital organs (hearts, kidneys, livers, etc.) may be harvested with impunity. Accordingly, explicit direction in your Health

---

[6] See http://www.cmri.org/03-terri-schiavo.shtml for more information.

[7] In your author's opinion, the same principles that inform the maintenance of a feeding tube under certain circumstances apply equally as well to the maintenance of a ventilator. In both cases, the living person processes the food/water or oxygen being supplied, not the machines. Thus, the treatment of a ventilator in a Health Care Proxy should parallel that of a feeding tube.

[8] Recall Lazarus in the tomb.

[9] For example, see this article http://www.traditioninaction. org/Cultural/E025cpDonor_1.htm, the website http://www. lifeguardianfoundation.org/, and the numerous articles at the *LifeSite News* (https://www.lifesitenews.com/) on the topic.

Care Proxy against organ donation is best. Short of that, organ donation should be limited to nonvital organs. You can direct that the donated organs must be used only for purposes that the Church has approved.

Closing out this chapter, here are some additional suggestions for the Health Care Proxy:

1. Express a preference for death at home rather than in an institution.
2. Reject treatments derived from organs/tissues of aborted children.
3. Reject embalming. This insult to the former (and future) temple of the Holy Ghost is not required by law in most cases.[10]
4. Reject autopsy (for the same reasons).

In the next chapter, we will deal with funeral and burial instructions, including suggestions for ensuring those instructions are carried out.

---

[10] See http://www.traditioninaction.org/Cultural/A046cpCivility Funeral 1.htm for more details.

CHAPTER 2

The Health Care Proxy: After Death

And now, children, hear me, and do not
stay here: but as soon as you shall bury your
mother by me in one sepulchre, without delay
direct your steps to depart hence.

—Tobias 14:12

In the last chapter, we focused on the time leading up to and immediately following death. In this chapter, funeral and burial wishes will take center stage followed by some ideas on enforcement.

At the outset, it important to note that a last will and testament is *not* the best place to record funeral and burial wishes. By the time that the "reading of the will" occurs, it is usually too late. And since the authority of your agent under your Health Care Proxy terminates at your death, the Health Care Proxy is not a good choice for recoding your funeral and burial wishes either. Rather a separate writing is the best approach.

What are some wishes worth mentioning? Clearly, your desire for a Requiem Mass should be first and foremost. Give all of the details you see fit to specify. These could include the location of the Mass, the type of Mass (High Mass, *Missa Cantata*, Low Mass), the type of music for a High Mass or *Missa Cantata* (Gregorian chant or polyphony), the priest to celebrate, the pallbearers, and requests for additional Masses (seventh day, thirtieth day, one-year anniversary of death or burial,[11] and/or Gregorian Masses[12]).

You may also wish to specify the type of casket you want. If cost is a concern, consider obtaining a very simple casket from a religious order.[13] Requesting a spiritual bouquet of Masses for your soul rather than flowers can be a good idea. Listing the Catholic cemetery you wish to be buried in also makes sense.

Be sure to mention your opposition to cremation, no matter what the alleged benefits are.[14] In doing so, think about

---

[11] All are taken from the useful form found here: https://lms.org.uk/sites/default/files/resource_documents/funeral-guide-jan-2014.pdf.

[12] See http://www.traditioninaction.org/religious/d014rp30Gregorian_Somerville.html for more information.

[13] These include the Benedictine monks of St. Joseph Abbey (http://www.saintjosephabbey.com/view-the-caskets/) or the Trappist monks of New Malleray Abbey (https://trappistcaskets.com/caskets/). The savings can be so substantial that in 2011, the Louisiana State Board of Embalmers and Funeral Directors sued the monks of St. Joseph Abbey, seeking to shut them down for selling caskets without a funeral directing license. Fortunately, the monks won.

[14] The alleged benefits, which include lower cost, less wasted space, portability of remains, and psychological finality, are refuted here: http://introiboadaltaredei2.blogspot.com/2016/12/the-evil-of-cremation.html.

citing past condemnations of the burning of corpses, including those of Pope Leo XIII ("detestable abuse"[15]), the 1917 Code of Canon Law ("reprobated"[16]), and the Holy Office ("barbarous practice"[17]).[18]

If you are concerned about your funeral and burial wishes being ignored, here are a few suggestions. First, explore whether a "Designation of Funeral Representative (DFR)" is available in

---

[15] On May 19, 1886, and on December 15, 1886, the holy office decreed against joining societies that promote the practice of burning the corpses of men and against commanding that one's own corpse or the corpses of others be burned. In confirming this decree to the ordinaries, Pope Leo XIII "ordered that they opportunely have the faithful of Christ instructed on the detestable abuse of cremating human bodies, and that with all their might they deter the flock entrusted to them from this (practice)." See Denzinger, *The Sources of Catholic Dogma* (Fitzwilliam, NH: Loreto Publications, 2004; Imprimatur, 1955), paragraph 1863 (pp. 465–66), footnote 1.

[16] Canon 1203.

[17] Instruction of the Holy Office to all bishops, June 19, 1926. See the full text here: http://www.cmri.org/03-cremation_holy_office.html. See http://www.cmri.org/03-cremation.html and http://www.cmri.org/03-cremation_not_for_caths.html and http://novusordowatch.org/2016/11/vatican-reminder-cremation-permitted/ for additional information.

[18] The following excerpt from Fr. Laux might also be used: "On December 8, 1869, the International Congress of Freemasons imposed it as a duty on all its members to do all in their power to wipe out Catholicity from the face of the earth. Cremation was proposed as a suitable means to this end, since it was calculated to gradually undermine the faith of the people in 'the resurrection of the body and life everlasting.'" Fr. John Laux, *Catholic Morality* (Imprimatur, 1932), p. 106.

your state.[19] A DFR allows you to confer on your appointee the authority to make decisions about your funeral arrangements and the disposition of your body. The appointee need not be a family member. Therefore, if none of your family members are on the same page as you with respect to your funeral and burial wishes (or if some are but live too far away), you can appoint a priest or a trusted friend as your representative.

Second, since *all things obey money*,[20] use your will to *disincentivize* your heirs from disregarding your wishes by staking a portion of their inheritance on it. This can be done with or without a DFR (or its equivalent). *To make this work, however, your heirs must be notified prior to your death of both your wishes and the provision in your will backing those wishes up.*

Here is an example.

> *If in the judgment of Fr. _____, my funeral and burial wishes were not satisfactorily complied with, $_____ shall be deducted from each of my heirs' inheritances. The aggregate of such reductions shall be distributed to _____ Catholic church for Masses to be said for _____.[21] The decision of Fr. _____ in this matter shall not be appealable to any court. Rather it shall be final*

---

[19] "Designation of Funeral Representative" is the name given to this legal instrument in Michigan. It may not be available in a particular state, or if it is, it may (as with the Health Care Proxy) go by a different name. Even if a DFR is not available in a particular state, one should be able to implement its equivalent with the assistance of legal counsel.

[20] Ecclesiastes 10:19.

[21] Add your own intention here. For example, you could add, "For those souls most in need of Our Lord's mercy."

> *and binding on all concerned. I recognize that if Fr. _____ is affiliated with _____ Catholic church at the time his decision is to be made, a potential conflict of interest may be created. I consider such a conflict of interest to be in appearance only. I fully trust that Fr. _____ will make an impartial decision.*

In the next chapter, we will look at the Durable Power of Attorney and some provisions that might be included in it.

CHAPTER 3

The Durable Power of Attorney

He made him master of his house, and
ruler of all his possession.
That he might instruct his princes as himself.
—Psalm 104:21–22

In this chapter, the document that complements the Health Care Proxy takes center stage, namely the Durable Power of Attorney. Where the Health Care Proxy dealt with the care of your person, the Durable Power of Attorney deals with the care of your property during your incapacity.[22]

The arrangement recorded by the psalmist is a good example of a power of attorney. While mentally competent, Pharaoh designated Joseph to "stand in his shoes" when it came to the management of Pharaoh's property (all of Egypt). If Joseph's authority had been deferred until Pharaoh's incapacity, this would have been a *springing* power. However,

---

[22] Since living trusts are also used for incapacity planning, the ideas discussed in this chapter are also applicable to them.

Joseph's authority was immediate upon his accepting the appointment. This made it an *immediate* power.

Another aspect of the arrangement was the *time limit* on Joseph's authority. What if Pharaoh became incapacitated sometime after the appointment was made? Would Joseph's authority *endure*? We are not told. However, if Joseph's authority did endure after Pharaoh's incapacity, it would have been a *durable* power of attorney. If not, it would have been a nondurable power. However, even if it was durable, Joseph's authority would certainly have expired at Pharaoh's death. The same is true today.

When it comes to estate planning, immediate Durable Powers of Attorney are generally preferable to springing durable powers. By appointing a master and ruler of all of your possessions in advance of your incapacity, your loved ones will not need to go to probate court (sometimes called a living probate) to get the authority to instruct your financial institutions and others on your behalf.[23]

Here are some recommendations. First, be sure to include among the standard authorizations a specific power to continue charitable giving. Without this, all giving—whether to charities or to family members—has to stop when you are incapacitated. For example, if you have been a longtime supporter of the poor and if you want your support to continue through your incapacity, you must say so in your Durable

---

[23] Remember, however, that after your death your agent has no authority to transfer your property to your heirs. To avoid having to go to probate court to obtain that authority (sometimes called a death probate), one or more of the following must be used: living trusts, joint tenancies with rights of survivorship, transfer of death/pay on death instructions, beneficiary (aka "lady bird") deeds, and/or beneficiary designation forms (typically used with annuities, life insurance, IRAs, and other retirement plans).

Power of Attorney. If you do not, the historical record of your generosity will do nothing to help.

Here is an example of how such a specific charitable giving power might read.

> *I authorize my agent to make charitable gifts as my agent believes I would make if I were able. I specifically give my agent the authority (i) to make qualified charitable distributions from one or more of my traditional IRAs to one or more qualified charitable organizations[24] and (ii) to accelerate testamentary charitable bequests (including testamentary charitable trusts or gift annuity arrangements) if this acceleration would be of greater benefit to me or my heirs.[25] [26]*

---

[24] Donors who are seventy and a half or older can give up to $100,000 from their IRAs (whether originally owned or inherited) directly to one or more charities. This is called a "qualified charitable distribution" or QCD. With QCDs, not only are income taxes avoided, but the donor's distribution obligation for the year is satisfied.

[25] Charities that accept governmental support should be viewed with suspicion because governmental support tends to cause mission drift. For example, in the 1971 Supreme Court case *Tilton v. Richardson*, to legally receive federal funds for the construction of new buildings on their campuses, four Catholic colleges had to present evidence that "there had been no religious services or worship in the federally financed facilities, that there are no religious symbols or plaques in or on them, and that they had been used for nonreligious purposes." In approving the federal grants, the court found that "[t]here is no evidence that religion seeps into the use of any of these facilities."

[26] To learn how much governmental support a charity receives, consult line 1e of Part VIII (Statement of Revenue) of its IRS Form

Second, if authorization for giving to family members will be granted, your agent might be tempted to make transfers to others to make you look "poor on paper" and qualify you for Medicaid.[27] You can head off that temptation with this provision.

> *The authority that I have given in this instrument to make gifts to my family members includes the authority to engage in so-called "Medicaid planning" but not for the sole purpose of preserving my heirs' inheritances if I am otherwise able to afford my own care. Rather, such planning shall only be undertaken to enhance the quality of my care or to protect my spouse from impoverishment, the preservation of my heirs' inheritances being only an incidental consequence thereof.*

In closing, consider whether the following legal estate planning maneuvers may also present some moral problems:

1. arranging the non-probate, non-living trust transfer of assets to heirs to evade the claims of legitimate creditors who, under the law of your state, may only satisfy their claims out of your of your probate and living trust estates;
2. claiming a valuation discount for gifts of business interests to family members on the grounds that (i)

---

990 (2017 version). Although by law, a charity must provide its Form 990 to anyone who asks for it, you can easily obtain a copy at http://www.guidestar.org/Home.aspx.

[27] "Do no fraud" (Mark 10:19).

there is no market for the interests (though their sale is never intended) and (ii) the recipients cannot exercise control (though control by the family as a whole is still maintained); and/or

3. setting property aside in so-called "asset protection trusts" so that the assets held by the trust are available to you but not to your creditors if you did something wrong.

This concludes our discussion of the Durable Power of Attorney. In the next chapter, we will examine the last will and testament, starting with some suggestions for an appropriate Catholic preamble.

CHAPTER 4

Last Will and Testament: Catholic Preamble

For where there is a testament,
the death of the testator must of necessity come in.
For a testament is of force, after men are dead:
otherwise it is as yet of no strength,
whilst the testator liveth.
—Hebrews 9:16–17

In the last chapter, we covered the Durable Power of Attorney. That instrument and the Health Care Proxy only have force when you are alive. After your death they have no strength because the authority of the appointed agents expires. Now, however, we will turn our attention to the legal instrument that takes over upon death, namely the last will and testament.

In past times wills covered only the disposition of real property (e.g., land, residences) and testaments covered only the disposition of personal property (e.g., jewelry) at death. Nowadays the distinction is no longer made. In fact, except in the heading, the word *testament* is rarely used in a will.

It is important to distinguish other documents that might

also include the word *will* in their names. For example, we saw that Living Wills are concerned with your health care during your incapacity, not your property after your death.

Ethical wills are gaining in popularity. Their focus is the transmission of spiritual goods at death (such as advice on how to live a good life,[28] hopes and dreams for the future, explanations of past events, expressions of love, requests for forgiveness,[29]

---

[28] For example, "I most warmly enjoin my children that, after what they owe to God, which should come first, they should remain forever united among themselves, submissive and obedient to their mother, and grateful for all the care and trouble which she has taken with them, as well as in memory of me. I beg them to regard my sister as their second mother. I exhort my son, should he have the misfortune of becoming king, to remember he owes himself wholly to the happiness of his fellow citizens; that he should forget all hates and all grudges, particularly those connected with the misfortunes and sorrows which I am experiencing; that he can make the people happy only by ruling according to laws: but at the same time to remember that a king cannot make himself respected and do the good that is in his heart unless he has the necessary authority, and that otherwise, being tangled up in his activities and not inspiring respect, he is more harmful than useful." The last will and testament of King Louis XVI is available at http://www.andrewcusack.com/2006/the-last-will-and-testament-of-louis-xvi/.

[29] For example, "I beg my wife to forgive all the pain which she suffered for me, and the sorrows which I may have caused her in the course of our union; and she may feel sure that I hold nothing against her, if she has anything with which to reproach herself." *Id.* The life of this most Christian King of France and his stance against "religious liberty," which cost him his life, are well worth learning more about. Pope Pius VI's *Quare Lacrymae* (1793) makes the case for Louis's martyrdom here: https://thejosias.com/2015/01/29/pius-vi-quare-lacrymae/.

etc.).[30] Although this can be done within the will proper, it is more commonly done in a separate document (or audio or video recording).

In her *Mystical City of God*, the venerable Mary of Agreda records the last will and testaments of our Lord and our Lady.[31] [32]

What should you say in your will? For an excellent start (sometimes called the preamble), you can declare your Catholic faith. We have some great examples from the past, including the following two:

Catholic Preamble for Will—Example 1

> *In the name of the Very Holy Trinity, Father, Son and Holy Ghost.*
>
> *I leave my soul to God, my creator; I pray Him to receive it in His mercy, not to judge it according to its merits but according to those of Our Lord Jesus Christ who has offered Himself as a sacrifice to God His Father for us other men, no matter how hardened, and for me first.*

---

[30] Chapter 4 of the book of Tobias contains an excellent example of an ethical will. It begins with these words: "Therefore when Tobias thought that his prayer was heard that he might die, he called to him Tobias his son, And said to him: Hear, my son, the words of my mouth, and lay them as a foundation in thy heart."

[31] Our Lord's will begins at paragraph 688 at http://www.neemcog.com/index_files/6TransfixionChXXII_nee.pdf.

[32] Our Lady's Will begins at paragraph 723 at http://www.neemcog.com/index_files/8CoronationChXVIII_nee.pdf.

I die in communion with our Holy Mother, the Catholic, Apostolic, Roman Church, which holds authority by an uninterrupted succession, from St. Peter, to whom Jesus Christ entrusted it; I believe firmly and I confess all that is contained in the creed and the commandments of God and the Church, the sacraments and the mysteries, those which the Catholic Church teaches and has always taught.

I pity with all my heart our brothers who may be in error but I do not claim to judge them, and I do not love them less in Christ, as our Christian charity teaches us, and I pray to God to pardon all my sins.[33]

Catholic Preamble for Will—Example 2

Prostrate in all humility, in the belief that God is in all places, sole being and creator of all immortal souls, with true knowledge of my own nothingness and impotence without His grace, I humbly implore His mercy on my misery, which has made me guilty of so much ingratitude for His goodness. I have offended this goodness by my sins, thus becoming unworthy to participate in the merits of Jesus crucified. Yet in these merits I place all my hope, and supplicate the Holy Virgin to be a true Mother to me and obtain

---

[33] You can read the last will and testament of King Louis XVI at http://www.andrewcusack.com/2006/the-last-will-and-testament-of-louis-xvi/.

for me pardon for the abuse I have made of the grace of God. To the moment of my death, and subject to the good pleasure of God, I supplicate my good angel guardian, Saint Louis, and all the saints to help me by their intercession in this important passage to which I submit myself, and were I not obliged thereto, for the love of God, and to honor the moment of the separation of the divine soul of my Savior, who desires my salvation, that I may glorify Him eternally with the Father and the Holy Ghost.

I protest before God, and before all creatures, that I wish to live and die in the Holy Roman Catholic and Apostolic Church, and I command my son, as far as I can, to do the same, it being the only path to paradise for which we were created. In the hope that God will grant him this grace, I beseech His bounty to take full possession of all that he is, to do in him and with him His most holy will. I likewise pray Him to pour out His most efficacious grace, for time and eternity, the blessing which, as mother, He has empowered me to give, and which I now give him: in the name of the Father, and of the Son, and of the Holy Ghost, Amen. I implore the sacred humanity of our Savior to have pity on our sinful souls at the hour of our death.

I also most humbly ask pardon of all my dear neighbors whom I have disedified or scandalized by my sins, of those whom I have displeased or offended in any way whatever, and of all creatures of which I have made bad use or contrary to the holy will of God. I abandon myself to God to make such restitution in this world or the next as it will please His merciful justice to ordain.[34]

Good luck to you (or your attorney) in trying to draft something that tops these two preambles! Nonetheless, after you've gotten your preamble down, it's time to appoint executors and more importantly for the parents of minor children, guardians. In the next chapter, we will focus on the latter. We will also take a look at other will-based arrangements that you can make for the Catholic upbringing of your children.

---

[34] See the last will and testament of Saint Louise de Marillac. This saint concludes her will in an exemplary way. "Behold, O my God, your poor creature, prostrate at the feet of Your grandeur and majesty! Acknowledging herself a criminal and deserving of hell, to which Your strict justice would have condemned me, were it not for the immense love which made Your son become man to deliver me. May it please Your divine majesty that I, with my son, be among the number of those who through Your son will eternally glorify You! Deign to look kindly on the acts, desires, and dispositions made in this will, drawn up in the belief that such is Your Divine Will, which has always directed mine, and without which I protest with all my strength never to will anything, and in which, I affirm, I wish to terminate my life, as I have this writing, which I have done and signed with my own hand, this Friday, the fifteenth day of December, 1645." The entire will, including the appointment of St. Vincent de Paul as the executor, can be found here: http://via.library. depaul.edu/cgi/viewcontent.cgi?article=1141&context=vhj.

CHAPTER 5

Last Will and Testament: Guardians

> As long as the heir is a child, he differeth
> nothing from a servant, though he be lord of
> all; But is under tutors and governors until
> the time appointed by the father.
>
> —Galatians 4:1–2

In the last chapter, we discussed the preamble to the last will and testament. In this chapter we will cover appointments of executors, who are the persons to carry out (or execute) the will's instructions,[35] and appointments of tutors and governors, who are the legal guardians who will raise minor children in their household. We will also take a look at arrangements

---

[35] If a living trust is being used, these would be the successor trustees. If the assets of the probate estate will be held in further trust, it is common to appoint the executors of the will as the trustees of those testamentary trusts.

that can be made under a will for the children's Catholic upbringing.[36]

When it comes to appointing executors, only those who are financially responsible, prudent, and trustworthy should be considered. As those who have accepted appointments to this role will readily attest, this is a job, not a privilege. On the other hand, the executor can subcontract some of the burden out to professionals and pay them out of estate assets. Doing this with the investment and tax-reporting functions is common.

As for appointing guardians, remember the most important duty that parents have under the fourth commandment—to pass the faith on to their children. One would think that if they were chosen for the right reasons, the children's spiritual parents— their baptism or confirmation sponsors—should be the leading candidates for the guardianship role. However, since it is possible for anyone to lose the faith, you can include the condition that the appointee agrees to raise the children Catholic.

Here is a sample provision.

> *I appoint as guardian of my minor children, my spouse (if living), or if my spouse is not living and has failed to appoint guardians for our minor children, I appoint _____ as guardian of my minor children. I appoint _____ to be the successor guardian of my minor children if and when all persons I have previously named shall fail to qualify or cease to act. No bond or other*

---

[36] Guardians are traditionally appointed only in wills, not living trusts. However, what is said in this chapter about financial arrangements for minor children applies equally to wills and living trusts.

> *security shall be required of any appointee.*
> *Each appointment made in this paragraph is*
> *on condition that the appointee promise that,*
> *to the best of his or her ability, he or she will*
> *ensure that my children will be well instructed*
> *in the Catholic religion, trained up as early as*
> *possible to a pious and virtuous life, guarded*
> *from being led into sinful or dangerous courses,*
> *and corrected with Christian charity.*[37]

With your children's spiritual welfare addressed, you can then cover their temporal needs. Trusts for their inheritances should be used to avoid the need for court appointed conservators.[38] Trusts should also be used to postpone the time of complete distribution of inheritances beyond the legal age of majority (typically age eighteen).

To avoid conflicts of interest, the trustee of the children's trusts should generally not be the children's guardian. In the

---

[37] The ideas that are contained in the last sentence of this sample provision were drawn from S. J. Deharbe's *A Complete Catechism of the Catholic Religion* (https://archive.org/details/completecatechis00deharich). Those wishing to elaborate further might consult *Lesson 33: Duties of Parents Toward Their Children* from Fr. Cogan's *A Brief Catechism For Adults: A Complete Handbook on How to Be a Good Catholic* (https://www.olrl.org/Lessons/).

[38] Of course, this assumes that your spouse does not survive you. If your spouse does survive you, it is assumed that all assets will pass under your will to your spouse. It might come as a surprise that you must make a will to ensure this result. If a will is not made (called dying *intestate*) and if the probate estate is large enough, the surviving spouse will have to share a portion of the probate estate with the children of the deceased spouse under the intestacy law of most states.

provisions describing when, how much, and for what purposes trust distributions to the children are to be made,[39] allowance should be given for payments to the guardian as well. Examples include reimbursement for payments made by the guardian on behalf of the children and for costs of enlarging the guardian's home to accommodate the children.

If you prefer that your children be raised in your home, be sure to authorize the trustee to cover the guardian's moving expenses. Also, be sure to authorize payment of the costs of maintaining and/or repairing the home while the guardian is there. Specifying that the guardian is not to pay rent is a must. Finally, allowing a reasonable time for the guardian to reside in the home while looking for a new residence after the guardianship ends (as well as covering the costs of relocation) also makes sense.

Given the longevity that many of our parents are enjoying these days, the possibility of our dying before them cannot be overlooked. In the next chapter, we will examine what may be done in a will to address this. We will also cover some other "pre-residuary gift" ideas.

---

[39] Here is one Catholic-minded example from the will of Ella C. Brady Deakyne, who died in 1941: "To pay the net income therefrom to Ruth M. Ogle of the City of Wilmington, Delaware, so long as she lives up to and observes and follows the teachings and faith of the Roman Catholic Church, and no longer; and upon her death, or failure to live up to, observe and follow the teachings and faith of that Church, as aforesaid, then and in that event the said principal sum of Ten Thousand Dollars, herein created as a Trust Fund, shall fall into, become, and be a part and portion of the said rest, residue and remainder of my estate, as set forth in and to be disposed of as herein provided." See *Delaware Trust Company v. Fitzmaurice*, 27 Del. Ch. 101 (Court of Chancery of Delaware, 1943). In 1941, when Ella died, $10,000 would be approximately $175,000 in today's dollars.

CHAPTER 6

Last Will and Testament: Pre-Residuary Gifts

Therefore, whilst we have time, let us work good to all men,
but especially to those who are of the household of the faith.
—Galatians 6:10

In the last chapter, we discussed arrangements for the spiritual and temporal welfare of minor children. This involved appointing appropriate guardians to raise them and worthy trustees to oversee their inheritances. In most cases, the children or trusts for their benefit (if they are minors) will be the recipients of the balance (or residue) of the estate.

Backing up a step, this chapter will consider what might be done in the way of pre-residuary gifts for parents, friends, and other members of the household of the faith. In the will document itself, these gifts typically come after the preamble and before the residuary clause. Here is an example.

> *I give $_____ to _____*
> *Catholic church for Masses to be said for my*
> *soul, for the soul of my deceased spouse, namely*

26

_____, *for the souls of my deceased parents, namely _____ and _____, and for the soul of my deceased child, namely _____. I give the residue of my estate to my children, in equal shares.*[40]

Although the options are endless, consider the following groups for gifts:

1. members of the clergy and other religious;[41]
2. godparents and godchildren;
3. chapels, seminaries, monasteries, and convents;
4. foreign missions;
5. Catholic elementary schools, high schools, and colleges;
6. funds for retired religious members;
7. funds for retired Catholic schoolteachers; and
8. Catholic newspapers, publishers, and websites.

If you are blessed to still have one or both of your parents still living and if your parent is dependent on you for financial

---

[40] Check with a member of the clergy for the details on the appropriate dollar limits and other rules applicable to bequests for masses for the dead. Also consider requesting Gregorian masses (http://www.traditioninaction.org/religious/d014rp30Gregorian_Somerville.html).

[41] Bear in mind that vows of poverty may prohibit a recipient from accepting your testamentary gift. In that case, consult with him or her to put together a workable alternative. Also bear in mind that if needed, no charitable deduction against the federal estate tax will be available for a distributions made directly to a member of a religious order (see chapter 9 for more information).

support, it makes sense to cover the possibility of your dying before your parent with a conditional gift, such as the following:

> *If I am survived by my mother, namely _____, then my executor shall set aside _____ percent of the value of my estate in a separate trust for my mother's benefit. This trust shall be held, administered, and distributed on the following terms: _____.*[42]

Using a trust for a parent makes more sense than an outright bequest for many reasons. First, the trust protects the assets from the undue influence of others. Second, it also avoids probate if your parent later becomes incapacitated. Third, a trust allows you and not someone else to decide who receives any assets that are left over when your parent dies.

Other parents include one's *alma mater* and *patria*. Concerning the former, a gift to a fund seeking the school's return to the Catholic faith may be more appropriate than a gift to the school itself.[43] Concerning your country, a gift in support of authentically Catholic missionary work in the US would be most *patriotic* of all. Paying federal estate taxes would be least so.[44]

---

[42] Be sure to include a provision in the trust to cover the costs of an appropriate funeral and burial (not cremation) for your parent. If you have been appointed guardian and/or conservator of a parent, be sure to check with local counsel on what might be done to appoint your successor.

[43] The Father King Society (Georgetown at http://www.gupetition. org/) and the Sycamore Trust (Notre Dame at https://sycamoretrust. org/) are examples.

[44] There's more on avoiding federal estate taxes in chapter 9.

Before we round out our discussion of pre-residuary gifts, a word on a relatively new development in the law of trusts (namely purpose trusts) would be appropriate. Before the purpose trust, there were private trusts and public trusts. The beneficiaries of private trusts make up a definite group of people, such as one's descendants. The beneficiaries of public trusts (also called charitable trusts) make up an indefinite number of people, such as the poor residing in a certain geographic area. In either case, *people* benefit.

With purpose trusts, however, *things* or *activities* are the beneficiaries. For example, a purpose trust could be established to construct and maintain a grave or monument; to support the saying of Masses; to maintain a church building, an organ, one or more statues, relics, or works of art; to support the Catholic press, both paper and internet, etc. Thus, as long as the purpose is legal, a trust can now be set up to support it after you are gone. And in certain states, there in no time limit on how long a purpose trust can last.[45] Here is a sample provision.

---

[45] When compared to charitable trusts, purpose trusts have at least three advantages. The first is privacy. Charitable trusts are generally formed with exemption from federal estate and income taxes in mind. But these exemptions require that the tax returns of the charitable trust be made available to anyone who asks for them. This is not the case with purpose trusts since purpose trusts cannot qualify for these tax exemptions anyway. The second advantage is that purpose trusts can support or oppose candidates in political campaigns. Charitable trusts that do this will lose their tax exemption. Third, when compared to a gift directly to a charity earmarked for the desired purpose, purpose trusts provide greater asset protection. If a legal judgment is obtained against the charity, the gift could be lost. This is not that case with a purpose trust since the assets of the purpose trust are not owned by the charity. This means that those assets are beyond the reach of the charity's creditors.

Upon my death, $_____
shall be held in separate trust, which shall be
administered and distributed as follows. Until
the Termination Date (defined below), the
trustee shall pay so much of the net income
and principal, even to the extent of exhausting
principal, as the trustee determines from time
to time to be desirable for the following purpose:

_____.

During the term of this trust, (a) the trustee
shall add any undistributed net income to
principal, and (b) my primary concern is
for the purpose described in the preceding
sentence, and the trustee need not consider
the interest of any remainder beneficiary in
making expenditures for that purpose. If the
trustee fails to carry out the terms of this trust,
_____ [46] shall have the
right and authority to enforce the terms of
this trust. Upon the earlier of (a) the purpose
for which this trust was established becoming
impossible or impracticable to fulfill or (b)
the expiration of the maximum period of
time allowed by law for a trust of this kind
to last (the Termination Date), the trust shall
terminate, and the trustee shall distribute
the remaining accumulated net income and
principal to _____.

---

[46] Name an individual on this line. If a long-term purpose trust is envisioned, include provisions to allow the named individual to nominate his or her successor.

In the next chapter, we will focus on planning for the residue of the estate, starting with a more detailed look at trusts for children.

CHAPTER 7

Last Will and Testament: Residuary Bequests for Children

But without faith it is impossible to please God.
—Hebrews 11:6

In the last chapter, we discussed "pre-residuary gift" ideas. These are the smaller, "off the top" gifts that are commonly made to favorite charities, side relatives, friends, or even purpose trusts. In this chapter, we will turn our attention to the balance (or residue) of the estate.

A somewhat common estate planning maxim on residuary bequests says, "There are three potential recipients—children,[47] Congress (estate taxes), and charity. You get to pick two."

For married couples, this "three Cs" maxim only applies at the second death because bequests to surviving spouses

---

[47] The ideas contained in this chapter are equally applicable to residuary bequests for grandchildren, nieces and nephews, and others.

who are US citizens are 100 percent estate tax deductible. Normally, the spousal bequest is made outright. However, if there is concern about protecting children's inheritances in case of remarriage or if there is a desire to protect the surviving spouse against fortune hunters, a bequest in trust could make more sense.

Even at the second death, the chances of Congress (or its collection agent, the IRS) becoming an heir is small. This is because the first $10 million (adjusted for inflation) of every estate is exempt from the federal estate tax. Accordingly, we will share a discussion of estate tax reduction strategies ("choosing children and charity over Congress" or "disinheriting the IRS") in the next chapter.

As with surviving spouses, outright bequests to children are the first option. By delivering the inheritance free of any trust, annual trustee and other fees are avoided. On the other hand, if the children are minors, if there is a prodigal in the family, or if there is merely a desire to keep the family assets in the family, a bequest in trust will be needed.

The fun part about trust-based bequests to children (at least from the parents' point of view) is that the parents get to write the rules. Directing the trustee to distribute income or principal[48] as needed for the children's health, education, maintenance, and support is very common. For Catholics, the health and education portions might be *baptized* with a supplemental provision like this:

> *For purposes of this instrument, "health" does not include the costs of a direct abortion; artificial insemination/fertilization/surrogate*

---

[48] Income is the fruit of the tree (dividends, interest, rents), and principal is the tree itself (stocks, bonds, rental real estate).

> *motherhood; contraception; vasectomy, tubal ligation, and any other form of direct sterilization; gender change; nontherapeutic plastic surgery; tattoos or body piercing; and any other practice condemned as sinful by the Catholic church.*[49]

> *For purposes of this instrument, "education" does not include any costs associated with studies that are contrary to Roman Catholic faith and morals. Conversely, generosity shall be shown where the following items are concerned, provided that they are authentically Catholic: pilgrimages, retreats, missions, seminary classes, home study courses, home education for children, online courses, Bibles, catechisms, other books (especially those written by or about the fathers of the Church and/or the Saints), newspapers, magazines, audios, and videos.*

Even with provisions like these, implementing a veto procedure makes sense, especially if a bank or other institution will be the trustee.

> *Notwithstanding the foregoing, the trustee shall not make any distribution to any beneficiary without giving _____ notice in writing at least thirty (30) days*

---

[49] According to *IRS Publication 502, Medical and Dental Expenses* (https://www.irs.gov/pub/irs-pdf/p502.pdf), abortion, birth control bills, in vitro fertilization, and sterilization (including vasectomies) are all tax deductible *health* expenses.

> *before making any such distribution and,*
> *if _____ gives written*
> *notice to the trustee not to make the intended*
> *distribution, the intended distribution*
> *shall not be made. The foregoing shall*
> *also apply to an individual appointed by*
> *_____ to be the successor*
> *possessor of this veto power. It shall also apply to*
> *such appointee's appointed successor and so on.*[50]

Incentive provisions may appeal to parents who want to put special emphasis on keeping the faith. For example, the trustee might be instructed to make a nominal distribution upon a child's first Holy Communion, confirmation, marriage (and anniversary thereof), or ordination (and anniversary thereof).

Other good behaviors that might be incentivized in this way include the periodic recitation of any one or more of the following:

1. baptismal vows,[51]
2. the oath against modernism,[52]

---

[50] On the blank lines, insert the name of a trusted member of the clergy or other trusted individual.

[51] See http://www.newadvent.org/cathen/02275a.htm and http://www.sanctamissa.org/en/resources/books-1962/rituale-romanum/09-baptism-of-children.html.

[52] "I... firmly embrace and accept each and every definition that has been set forth and declared by the unerring teaching authority of the Church, especially those principal truths which are directly opposed to the errors of this day. And first of all . . ." (http://www.papalencyclicals.net/Pius10/p10moath.htm). See also http://www.cmri.org/95prog9.htm.

3. the Athanasian creed,[53]
4. the pledge of the legion of decency,[54] and
5. the profession of faith by a convert[55].

Regular performance of one or more of the corporal/spiritual works of mercy[56] or of the commandments of the church[57] might likewise be encouraged.

Sinful behavior might be *disincentivized* by allowing distribution of income only (and no principal) until the sinful behavior ceases. Or one could cut off both income and principal unless there is dire need.[58]

Lastly, here are some other ideas to consider when planning trust-based residuary bequests for children.

---

[53] "Whosoever will be saved, before all things it is necessary that he hold the Catholic Faith. Which Faith except everyone do keep whole and undefiled, without doubt he shall perish everlastingly. And the Catholic Faith is this . . ." (http://www.newadvent.org/cathen/02033b.htm).

[54] A more updated version can be found here (red text at bottom). http://introiboadaltaredei2.blogspot.com/search?q=legion+of+decency.

[55] "I, N. N. ... years of age, born outside the Catholic Church, have held and believed errors contrary to her teaching. Now, enlightened by divine grace, I kneel before you, Reverend Father..." (http://www.sanctamissa.org/en/resources/books-1962/rituale-romanum/61-appendix-reception-of-converts-profession-of-faith.html).

[56] See http://www.newadvent.org/cathen/10198d.htm.

[57] See http://www.newadvent.org/cathen/04154a.htm.

[58] In this case, the income could either be accumulated in the trust for later distribution when the sinful behavior stops or be distributed to charity as long as the sinful behavior continues. The latter will save significant federal and state trust income taxes.

1. Never condition a distribution on a child's entering into a prenuptial agreement. This makes the child choose between an inheritance and a valid marriage.

2. Anticipate a child's possible renouncement of all or a portion of the inheritance (called a disclaimer) by providing an alternative beneficiary, such as a favorite charity.

3. Temper the ability of spendthrift clauses to protect trust assets against creditors. While meant to protect prodigals against themselves,[59] these clauses have worked too well in some cases, resulting in courts siding with the trustees of (and against the victims of) child molesters, murderers, and deadbeat dads.

4. Implement a Catholic investment policy for trust funds. While never perfect, an honest attempt at avoiding profit from sin gives a much better example than silence.

5. Consider including an arbitration clause to keep disputes out of court.[60]

6. If you permit loans from the trust to children or you encourage them instead of distributions, make sure that they make repayment without interest (usury).[61]

In the next and final chapter, we cover how charitable giving can be used to legally disinherit the IRS as an heir of your estate.

---

[59] Without a spendthrift (or anti-alienation) clause, a prodigal who is denied a distribution by a trustee can indirectly obtain money by selling his trust interest or pledging it for a loan. In some states, such a New York, a spendthrift clause is assumed, even if the trust instrument itself is silent.

[60] "Dare any of you, having a matter against another, go to be judged before the unjust, and not before the saints?" (1 Corinthians 6:1).

[61] In other words, require that nothing more than the original loan be repaid. "Lend, hoping for nothing thereby" (Luke 6:35).

CHAPTER 8

Last Will and Testament: Residuary Bequests to Charity

Render therefore to Caesar the things that are Caesar's.
—Mathew 22:21

In the last chapter, the "children, Congress, and charity" maxim was introduced, and the focus was on residuary bequests to Children. Because of the currently high federal estate tax exemptions, which make the federal estate tax irrelevant for most of us,[62] we postponed a discussion of how charitable giving can be used to disinherit the IRS by choosing

---

[62] Under the Tax Cuts and Jobs Act, which was signed into law on December 22, 2017, the federal estate tax exemption for the estates of those dying in 2018 through 2025 is $10 million indexed for inflation. For the estates of those dying in 2026 and later years, the exemption returns to its pre-2018 level of $5 million indexed for inflation. Since each estate enjoys its own exemption, the total amount that can be sheltered from federal estate tax by a married couple (two estates) is twice the exemption amount.

children and charity over Congress. We now pick up from where we left off.

The federal estate tax is a voluntary tax. In other words, you don't have to render anything to Caesar if you don't want to. The unlimited deduction for charitable bequests makes this possible. To illustrate, assume that Joseph, a widower with three children, has an $11 million estate. Joseph dies in 2018, leaving his entire estate to his children. To keep the math simple, assume that the federal estate tax exemption applicable to Joseph's estate is $10 million. (In reality, the exemption would be higher because of inflation indexing.) Joseph's children would inherit $10.6 million, Congress would take $400,000 (40 percent of the $1 million by which $11 million exceeds the $10 million exemption), and charity would get zero. Let's call this plan A.

However, if Joseph leaves his federal estate tax exemption to his children and the balance to charity (plan B), the children would get $10 million, charity would get $1 million, and Congress would get zero.[63] With plan B (commonly called a "zero estate tax plan"), Joseph has voluntarily chosen to

---

[63] If Joseph's traditional IRA or other traditional retirement plan formed a portion of the assets passing to charity, all the better. Not only would all federal estate taxes on the IRA be eliminated, but all federal income taxes too.

disinherit the IRS by choosing children and charity over Congress.[64] To summarize, you can consult the following table:

	Children	Charity	Congress
Plan A	$10.6 million	$-0-	$400,000
Plan B	$10 million	$1 million	$-0-

A provision to implement a zero estate tax plan might say the following:

> *I give the smallest amount necessary to eliminate all federal estate taxes on my estate to _____.[65] I give the balance of my estate to my children in equal shares.*

It should be noted that bequests to members of the clergy and members of religious orders are not estate tax deductible. For example, in the *Callaghan* case,[66] Margaret E. Callaghan died in 1952, leaving her estate equally to her four children, two of whom were nuns. Although each sister was obligated by her vow of poverty to relinquish her inheritance to her convent, the tax court ruled that the bequests to the two nuns

---

[64] If Joseph had wanted his entire $11 million estate to pass estate tax free to his children, he might have established an irrevocable trust to own a $1 million life insurance policy on himself. That way, at his death, his children would receive $10 million estate tax free from his estate *plus* another $1 million estate tax free from the irrevocable trust ($11 million total). Charity would still receive $1 million, and Congress would still receive nothing.

[65] Insert names of charities here.

[66] 33 T.C. 870 (1960).

were not tax deductible. Had Margaret given directly to the two convents, $24,700[67] in estate taxes would have been saved.

It should also be noted that even bequests to family-run charities (called private foundations) are fully deductible. Thus, in Joseph's case, if the $1 million went to Joseph's private foundation, the federal estate tax would still be zero, even though the children would have complete control over how foundation assets were invested and spent.[68] And since there are no time limits on how long private foundations can last, Joseph's grandchildren could take it over after his children, his great-grandchildren after his grandchildren, and so on through all future generations.

Before closing, two other charitable giving techniques are worth a brief mention. The first is called a charitable remainder trust (CRT for short). CRTs first make payments to heirs, with the balance (or remainder) then passing to charity.[69] Leona Helmsley left a CRT to her grandchildren, but with a twist. Instead of being automatic, the yearly payments to the grandchildren were conditioned on their making an annual visit to the grave of Ms. Helmsley's late son (their father) and signing the registry placed there.[70] In that case, as with all other CRTs, the payments to the heirs are not estate tax deductible, but the payment to the charity is.[71]

---

[67] That's approximately $230,000 in today's dollars.

[68] The children could also pay themselves out of the foundation for their work without jeopardizing the deduction. Such compensation would, however, be subject to income tax.

[69] Sample provisions for this type of trust can be found at the IRS's website (https://www.irs.gov/irb/2005-34_IRB).

[70] Ms. Helmsley's will may be read at http://uniset.ca/misc/helmsley_will.html.

[71] This is the case even if the remainder charity is one's own private foundation.

The second technique is called a charitable lead trust (CLT for short). A CLT is the reverse of a CRT. Thus, payments are first made to charity (the *lead* beneficiary) with the balance then passing to heirs.[72] CLTs are sometimes called "Jackie O Trusts" because Jacqueline Kennedy Onassis's will contained one.[73] With CLTs, only the payments to charity are deductible against the estate tax.[74] However, if these payments are of a sufficient number and of a sufficient size, a CLT can be used to pass any estate, no matter how large, estate tax free to heirs.[75]

---

[72] Sample provisions for this type of trust can be found at the IRS's website (http://www.irs.gov/irb/2007-29_IRB/ar11.html and http://www.irs.gov/irb/2008-30_IRB/ar20.html).

[73] Ms. Onassis's will may be read at http://www.truetrust.com/Famous_Wills_and_Trusts/Jacqueline_Kennedy_Onassis_Will.html.

[74] This is the case even if the payments are made to one's own private foundation.

[75] In Joseph's case, if he had wanted his entire $11 million estate to pass estate tax free to his children *and* if he were uninsurable, he might have left the $1 million that would otherwise be subject to tax to a CLT. Although the children would have to wait a decade or two to receive this second installment of their inheritance, the initial $1 million and whatever it may have grown to by the time of the last payment to Joseph's foundation would pass to the children estate tax free.

Appendix

Case Study

Who is the Father of orphans... God in His holy place.
—Psalm 67:6

In this appendix, we will apply what we have learned to a case study involving a family of modest means but rich in children.[76]

Michael and Andrea have been blessed with eleven children—six boys and five girls. Mary (age twenty) is the oldest. Theresa (age eighteen) is the second oldest, and Abigail (age one) is the youngest. Michael is self-employed. Andrea works part-time when she can. The children attend Catholic school.

To prevent a court from placing Mary with one of their non-Catholic family members, Michael and Andrea prepared wills shortly after Mary was born. They appointed Mary's godparents as her guardians.[77]

---

[76] Your author owes a debt of gratitude for the helpful insights provided by the couple on whose actual circumstances this case study is based.

[77] Out of concern for possible complications during delivery, the couple had already prepared durable powers of attorney and health care proxies prior to Mary's birth.

Michael and Andrea included a testamentary trust for Mary in their wills.[78] Michael's brother John was named as trustee. John's atheism did not bother Michael and Andrea because as trustee, he would have no authority over Mary's upbringing. John's business acumen, however, would serve Mary's temporal interests well. Plus, the couple included the following provision, which John would have to follow as trustee:

> *The trustee shall employ the net income and principal of this trust in the education, maintenance, and support of our daughter, Mary, until she shall arrive at the age of twenty-five (25) years, but prior to that time, only so long as she is brought up and reared in the Roman Catholic faith. Said payments of net income and principal are to be made from time to time by the trustee to such persons and in such manner as the trustee, in his executive judgment may determine for Mary's best interests and in accordance with the terms of this trust, the trustee being restricted in his discretion during Mary's minority alone to this, that the trustee shall obtain once a year a certificate from the Roman Catholic school during Mary's attendance at school and a certificate from the Roman Catholic priest of the parish in which Mary resides that Mary is being brought up and reared in the Roman Catholic faith. Upon*

---

[78] Unlike a living trust, a testamentary trust does not avoid probate at death. However, at this stage in their lives, the young couple preferred the risk of a highly unlikely probate to paying more for a living trust to avoid it.

Mary's arriving at the age of twenty-five (25)
years, this trust shall terminate, and the trustee
shall distribute the remaining net income and
principal to Mary outright and free of trust.[79]

By the time Maximilian, the couple's eighth child, was born, however, Michael and Andrea had to confront some difficult questions. First, all of the children's godparents (four couples total serving in rotation) had either left the faith or lost touch with Michael and Andrea. Who should be guardians now? Second, was it reasonable to ask any couple—Catholic or not—to take eight children into their home? Third, where would the money to cover the costs of raising all the children come from?

---

[79] This is the nearly verbatim reproduction of the trust provision included in the last will and testament of Thomas Devlin for the benefit of his three-year-old grandson, Clarence, as quoted in the 1925 Pennsylvania Supreme Court case *Devlin's Trust Estate*, 284 P.A. 11, 130 A. 238 (1925). Thomas's Catholic son (Clarence's father) was already deceased at the time of Thomas's death. Overlooking the fact that prior to their marriage, Thomas's son and his Protestant fiancé, Sarah, had agreed that all of their children would be raised Catholic, upon Sarah's challenge, the court invalidated the provision on the grounds that it would compel Sarah to raise Clarence against her own faith and that it would cause disruption of the mother-child relationship. More simply, the court wasn't buying what it perceived to be a veiled attempt of a Catholic grandfather to force his non-Catholic daughter-in-law to raise his grandson Catholic as she had promised. Because this case is distinguishable in a number of ways from Michael and Andrea's case (trust created by both parents instead of by a grandparent; both parents Catholic instead of just one; both parents deceased instead of just one; guardian Catholic instead of non-Catholic), there is no reason to think a provision like this would be struck down again if challenged today.

Fortunately, the last question was the easiest to handle. Working with a good life insurance agent, Michael was able to obtain an affordable thirty-year-term life insurance policy on himself that, if invested conservatively after his death, could be expected to provide just enough to meet the children's temporal needs.[80] [81]

The first and second questions were harder. Trusting in the providence of the Father of orphans, the couple made the best guardian selections from their non-Catholic family members that they could, urging that the children be kept together if at all possible. The couple also vowed to redouble their efforts to strengthen their children in the faith *now* so as to inoculate them from potential bad example later.

---

[80] With this kind of policy, the coverage is valid only for the time (or term) specified and no longer. (In Michael and Andrea's case, the coverage was needed for the time the children would still be minors, allowing for the possibility of a few more new arrivals.) For example, if a thirty-year term policy is taken out in year 1 and if the insured dies in year 20, the policy's beneficiaries are entitled to the death benefit because the insured died during the term (between year 1 and year 30). On the other hand, absent further action, death after the term will result in no death benefit because the policy will have lapsed. Since the coverage is limited in this way and since we are living longer on average, term life insurance can be a very cost-effective way of providing funds to raise children *as long as the prospective insured is in good health at the time application for the policy is made.* In your author's opinion, parents of just about any means with just about any size family are well advised to *take prompt action* to secure an appropriate level of term coverage. Procrastination followed by an unexpected illness or accident could mean much higher premiums or no coverage at all.

[81] In the interest of full disclosure, your author possesses only a license to practice law, not one to sell life insurance or any other financial product.

As for the life insurance, family home, and other assets, the couple decided that the time had come to avoid probate with a living trust. To save trust administration costs, the assets would be held in a single common trust for the benefit of all eight children (as opposed to eight separate trusts, one for each child). The "Catholic upbringing" provision for Mary quoted previously was maintained but now broadened to include all of the children until the youngest reached age twenty-five. The following provision was also included to give preference to the younger children:

> *Without limiting the trustee's discretion, the trustee may consider the needs of a child who has not attained twenty-five (25) years of age as more important than the needs of a child who has attained that age.*

When Abigail arrived (bringing the total count up to the present eleven children), the guardianship problem had solved itself. Since Mary was now a legal adult, *she* could be named as guardian. Before revising their wills, however, Michael and Andrea informed Mary of the large responsibilities and complete disruption of her life that being guardian of her younger siblings would entail. Fortunately, Mary was up to the task. Michael and Andrea revised their wills accordingly. And to avoid repeat trips to their attorney, they included a provision that would automatically add their other children to the guardian list when they reached legal adulthood.

Printed in the United States
By Bookmasters